Table of Cont

About The Author

I have been a web designer for the past 14 years and for 10 of those years I have been self-employed. I started out working for a couple of the dot com businesses that sprouted up in the early 2000's and then moved on to working as a contractor for the Office of the Under Secretary of Defense in the Pentagon.

When the contract ended I made the decision to start a freelance web design business. I can still remember my first day. I had set-up my own home office and I sat in the corner staring at my computer screen. And there I sat having told my friends and family about my new business, having what felt like a real office and yet I had no work and quite frankly, I wasn't sure how to get any.

Looking back I'm very thankful I made the decision to start my own freelance web design business because it has truly changed my life. Instead of being paid an hourly rate I am now in more control of my income and I also have a lot more freedom since I am not tied to a desk for 8+ hours per day.

Although I'm very thankful for the experience I have had in learning how to get things started, I would have loved to have had someone to lean on who could give some direction so I didn't have to start from scratch. This book is my way of helping those who are getting started by giving them a jumpstart so it doesn't take as long to start earning money and to be able to experience the freedom and joy having your own freelance business can bring.

Good luck and to your success!

What This Book Is

Starting a web design business from home that earns you at least $1,000 per month is completely doable and I've written this book to be your guide and show you exactly how to make it happen.

I didn't write this book to tell you what you want to hear, I wrote this book to tell you what you need to know. This book isn't filled with a bunch of fluff to get you excited about the industry. Rather, I've filled it with real steps you will need to take to start earning $1,000+ per month.

I've been a web designer for over a decade now so you'd better bet I've worked with all different types of customers and personalities out there. I believe that experience is very important to share so we'll be spending a good deal of time talking about how to set-up a solid process for managing your projects and customers so you can dramatically reduce the number of problem clients you have, complete projects quickly and ultimately earn more money.

In the final section of this book you'll find example documents that you can tweak and use to get your business started including a list of questions to ask every customer, a sample web design proposal, a sample contract, project task checklist and several others.

What This Book Is Not

This book was written to teach you how to start a web design business. It was not written to teach you how to build websites. If you don't have experience in creating websites, I'll point you to some online courses were you can learn how to set-up websites with no coding and no experience so you can still get started this weekend.

I'm really excited to help take you through this journey. After you've finished going through this book and begin setting up your business, I encourage you to contact me if you have any questions or if I can help you in anyway. I'd love to hear from you and to offer support! Enough talking, let's get you on track to start earning $1,000 per month with your new web design business!

Home Web Design Business - Biggest Online Opportunity Today! Getting Started

The Basic Skills You'll Need to Succeed With Your Home Web Design Business

You may be surprised at what I'm going to say are the skills you need to be successful in this business. Your business savviness is way may important than your web design skills. That's right, your web design skills are not the most important. Don't worry, I'll explain what I mean here but first let me share with you the top three skills you will need to be successful in web design (in order of importance):

1. Great customer service

2. Great marketing skills

3. Web design creativity

This list may look backwards to you at first but here's why it's not. If you excel at customer service, you will excel in this business. Customers want to be listened to, they want to be acknowledged and they want to feel like you care. If you can do that, you'll have no problem earning at least $1,000 a month in your business. If you are the greatest designer in the world but you don't get back to your customers in a timely manner or you don't make them feel like you care about your work, it doesn't matter. They won't come back to you and they won't tell others anything positive about you.

A lot of people hesitate to get into this field because they lack confidence in their design skills. The truth is there are "designers" of all levels who make lots of money every month. Focus on your customer service and you'll excel. To get a bit more specific, here is what I have found makes for great customer service in the web design business:

▸ Responding to a Customer the same business day (or early the next day if they contacted you late in the business day)

▸ Informing the Customer of your progress before they are expecting an update

▸ Doing just a little something extra for them (we'll talk more about this later)

▸ Taking an extra few minutes to answer their questions and explain why you do things the way you do them (also makes for a smoother process)

- Asking them a personal question (how's business going for them, what did they do fun over the weekend, etc.). Just let them talk about themself for a few minutes.

Now this will work for 95% of your customers. And you can just forget about the other 5%. There is nothing you can do to please them anyway (and we'll definitely talk more about that later on).

You will of course need some marketing skills to succeed as well because you'll need to find customers initially to get you started. But again if you concentrate on providing great customer service there will be less and less marketing that you'll need to do down the road. In a future section we will talk more about marketing and how you can find your first customers to get you started towards earning at least a thousand dollars per month.

Do You Know Enough to Really Do This? Yes, You Do! This Will Surprise You!

Yes, absolutely. This is something you can do even if you don't know how to code. WHAT?! Let me repeat what I've already said. If you focus on providing great customer service and marketing the services you offer, you can excel at this.

I've included access to two online courses that teach you how to set-up websites without any experience or any coding required so you can really learn to do this in a weekend if you'd like to. To make it easier, you can also set-up a small team of freelancers who can support you with smaller tasks or even taking on full websites will you collect the profit. It's entirely up to you how to set this up.

Everything I've included in this book will help you to get set up this weekend so that you can begin providing web design services immediately. So let's get started!

Tools You'll Need (& How to Get Everything You Need for Free)

Starting a home web design business can be done completely for free - assuming you already have a computer and an internet connection. There are a few tools you'll need to get started.

This day in age, there are tons of pricey (although excellent) software out there but there are also very competitive, quality free tools available to you. Starting a home web design business doesn't and shouldn't put you in debt.

▸ GIMP (a photoshop alternative) - www.gimp.org

▸ Google Apps (lots of free and paid apps to help you run your business) - www.google.com/enterprise/apps/business/

▸ Wave Apps (free cloud accounting software) - www.waveapps.com

▸ WordPress (https://wordpress.org) and Joomla (www.joomla.org)

If you do not have experience creating websites and do not want to learn to code, see the special bonus section in this book for an online courses on how to set-up websites without any knowledge of coding.

If you're looking for a particular software, googling "open source software" + *type of software* will give you the results you need (as long as the software exists, of course). Don't forget to google "free alternative to [*insert name of Software, ie. - Photoshop*]".

Setting Up Your Own Website & 6 Elements It Must Have to Attract New Clients

Don't underestimate the importance of your own website. Before you even start thinking about getting started or building your portfolio, as we'll talk about shortly, focus on the website you will be using for your web design business. Remember, it's the first impression potential customers will have of your work. They will often see your website before they see your portfolio so don't skimp on your own website.

You don't need a huge website but there are a few key elements you'll want to make sure you include so let's look at what those are:

- A nice design

  Okay, duh! But seriously, not everyone thinks about this. Remember your website may be a potential customers first impression. You want to wow them as this is going to be a reflection of the quality of the website they'll get from you.

- An about you section

  This information shouldn't be on your homepage. Your homepage should be reserved for what services you offer and helping visitors access those services. Some people may want to know more about you though. Create an about page, include your picture and some information about you.

- An easy way for customers to contact you

  Another duh moment, right? I've seen plenty of designers not make this easy to do though. Make it obvious how visitors can contact you.

- Overview of your services

  Let new (and current) customers know about all of the services you offer. If you don't talk about it, no one will know you offer it.

- Examples of your work

  You must show off examples of your work if you expect anyone to hire you. Shortly we're going to be talking about how to quickly build your website portfolio if you don't already have one.

- An obvious call to action

  As with any website, you need to make it obvious what you want your website visitors to do. Think about what is most important and highlight that.

Remember your website is your biggest marketing material so don't try and cut corners here. I've heard many web designers talk about how outdated their own website is but I guarantee that is costing them more money than they realize. Schedule time to keep your own website up-to-date and attract more customers because of it.

The Biggest Secret to Success: Establishing Your Expertise

Finding a Niche to Make the Most Money From Your Web Design Business

When you are starting your business you have two options of who you'll serve:

1. Everybody and anybody
2. A select group (niche)

There are pros and cons to each but in my experience you'll be less stressed and make more money (that's what this is all about anyway, right?) in the long run. Having a successful web design business, as with any business, is going to require focus. The best thing that you can do to set yourself up for success is to focus on a particular niche. What do I mean by this? I mean select an industry that you would like to focus on. This will help you focus on your marketing efforts it will help you target specific leads and it will help establish you as an expert in that field.

So let's think about that for a moment. Let's say you operate a hair salon, you are going to be opening a new store and you are currently looking for a web designer to help you build your first website. Do you think you'll be more likely to go with a web designer who services anyone and everyone who comes to their door from someone selling auto parts to a food delivery service or a web designer who charges competitive rates compared to the previous designer but focuses solely on servicing hair salons and providing the features that they need to excel in their industry?

You'll without a doubt select the web designer who focuses on hair salons solely. This web designer not only knows web design but they understand your industry, they understand your competitors and they understand what features are needed on your website to help you excel online.

As you can see with this example, it will be a much, much easier sell when you are speaking with potential customers because you are an expert in serving their industry. This instantly makes them feel more comfortable with you and like they are in the right hands.

This will also set you apart from the endless number of web designers and web design companies out there as most of them do not focus. Simply put, you will be much more efficient at customer service and marketing and ultimately your revenue will be much higher than if you choose not to focus. But it's up to you!

If a particular industry does not jump out at you right away, open your phone book (do people still do that?) or just jump online and do a search for different types of companies in your area. Try going to https://local.yahoo.com, typing in your area and look through the business categories. You could focus on:

- Restaurants
- Auto Repair Shops
- Dentists
- Doctors
- Hair Salons & Barbers
- Real Estate Agents
- and so many others

Once you have selected your niche, it is much easier to set-up your web design packages, pricing and to create a list of plugins and/or extensions that you will be using on all (or at least most) of your websites. Ultimately, the website creation process will be more automated and will help you to finish your projects faster.

As we'll discuss more about, if you choose to outsource all or some of the work, focusing on one niche will help you to train your team and help them to finish their work faster as well.

Even more importantly, if you focus on a particular niche, you will be able to charge higher rates because of your "specialization" than a web designer who serves anyone and everyone.

5 Ways to Create a Portfolio Quickly and Easily If You Don't Already Have One

It will be difficult to get work if you don't have a portfolio you can show off. To get started, you really only need a handful of portfolio examples. Some companies that have been around for years don't show more than 10 examples. Don't feel pressured to come up with a dozen examples of your work before you start your business.

However many portfolio items you come up with, make sure you only include your best work. Quality over quantity is always better. It's better to have a few examples of some truly amazing work than it is to have a dozen examples of average work. If a customer is deciding whether or not to use your service, they can only expect for their website to be as good as the worst example in your portfolio so keep that in mind.

As you complete paid website work you will continue to grow your portfolio but keep quality in mind. I have completed many websites over the years where the customer was thrilled with the website but I personally didn't like it. I designed it to their taste so they were happy. There is nothing wrong with that but I certainly didn't add those sites to my portfolio.

With all that being said you have a couple of options for building your website portfolio quickly.

1. Approach business owners in the niche you are targeting and offer them a free website in exchange for a review, testimonial, etc.

2. Use Elance.com or Odesk.com and bid low on projects to find potential customers who care more about the price than your portfolio.

3. Create fake websites for fake customers so you can set websites up quickly.

4. If you're interested in helping a non-profit (or that's the niche you'll be getting into) check out https://www.catchafire.org/ where you can find non-profits in need of web design help.

5. Consider relationships you already have. If you want to target a restaurants or hair salons and you have one you frequent, approach the person who knows you there to see if you can pitch your service to them. People who know you or more likely to purchase from you even with little to no portfolio.

Setting Yourself Up For Success; How to Do Things Once That You Can Use Over and Over Again

The Secret to Establishing Prices & Creating Web Design Packages Customers Want

As you enter the web design business, get ready to be asked about your prices. In fact, that is one of the first things every customer is going to ask you - often before you even get into what it is that they're looking for. Many business owners simply view web design as an off-the-shelf product and expect you to provide a price immediately like it's a set of headphones or something. Some will struggle with the fact that *"it depends,"* as you'll tell them. With that being said, let's look at what and how you can charge your customers.

As you set your rates, stick to them. Don't let customers tell you what your rates are. No matter what rate you set, some people will think you're too cheap and some will think you're too expensive. That's with anything so stick to the rates you set. Remember your rate is not just about the website you will be delivering but it is about the *quality* of service you will be providing them as well. Remember that great customer service we've been talking about?

As I've already mentioned, one of the greatest things about specializing and servicing a particular niche is you can demand more money. As your experience and portfolio grow, you can continue to increase your rates. Why? Because you have become the go to person for anyone who works in this particular niche. People in the niche industry are going to want you not only because you specialize in their niche but because you will be referred by others in their industry. You are simply the person who knows their stuff and understands their industry the best. Nice, right?

Another benefit we haven't discussed for focusing on a particular niche is you can avoid doing a lot of custom work. Custom work involves incorporating functionality into a website that you don't incorporate for most websites you work on. It is unique to one customer. Although custom sites have a higher price tag, they also come with a lot more of a time investment on your part. There is more time involved in the initial stage of finding out what your customer wants, more time involved in researching what plugins/extensions are available and more time involved in actually setting up these unique features that you don't typically do.

Within a niche you will be able to establish a set of packages that most of your Customers can pick from. And by offering three packages, every customer will most likely select from the top two expensive ones. "Package" websites can be completed quickly and professionally for maximum profit. It is much easier to complete several package websites each month than it is to complete several custom websites.

If you offer three website packages, each package should build on the previous package and the price should increase along with the number of options included. As a basic example, your website packages could look something like this:

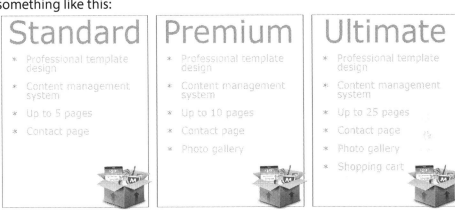

Standard	Premium	Ultimate
* Professional template design	* Professional template design	* Professional template design
* Content management system	* Content management system	* Content management system
* Up to 5 pages	* Up to 10 pages	* Up to 25 pages
* Contact page	* Contact page	* Contact page
	* Photo gallery	* Photo gallery
		* Shopping cart

See the appendix for a greater example of website packages you can tweak and use for your customers.

When it comes to pricing you have two options to consider: 1) charging by the hour or 2) charging by the project. Both have their pros and cons. Either way is okay, you'll just need to decide what works best for you. Let's talk about the pros and cons of each and then we can get more into specific pricing.

Charging By The Hour

Many web designers prefer to take the per hour approach as it's pretty straightforward. If they complete 20 hours of work, they simply multiple that by their hourly rate and tada - they have their invoice total.

Charging by the hour definitely has it's upsides. If you end up working with a Customer who continuously changes their mind you will be able to bill them for all the hours you've worked without having to get frustrated by their requests.

On the flip side, customers are not always thrilled when they cause your hours to go up. As customers request updates to your work they will 90% of the time ask for an estimate of time with this billing method. You'll have to take the time to send them an hourly estimate but note that this can sometimes turn into a discussion. A task can sometimes appear easier or less time consuming than it actually is and customers may question your estimate.

For the customers who don't care about money as much, doing a project by the hour can quickly turn into what may feel like a never ending project. The customer has you complete a feature, tries it and asks you to switch it to something "better." I guarantee after awhile this can get quite annoying and you'll want to move on to the next web design project.

Charging By The Project

One benefit of charging by the project is both you can the customer will know exactly what to expect. As the designer you can pad the price a little bit to cover any unforeseen work that could come up and for the customer, they will feel comfortable that you are not racking up the hours and running up their bill.

Some web designers have gotten creative and have taken the estimated number of hours needed to complete a project, multiplied it by their hourly rate and then added an additional 10% - 15% markup to protect them in case the customer wants something changed or requires more attention than normal. This can protect you from losing profit you're entitled to and you can even give the customer a discount if you finish up earlier than expected and nothing comes up. And you'd better bet that would make them a happy - and now loyal - customer!

Charging by the project can be difficult if you are outsourcing any of the work. If you do this I would recommend working with a freelancer who will charge you by the project as well so the price doesn't creep up on you. In order to make the most profit you have to be good at clearly defining the work (as you should have done in the proposal stage) and sticking to that, not allowing customers to continually change the scope of the project. It will simply be too costly for you.

So What Should You Do?

I'm not going to make this decision for you. You have to decide what works best for you, your business and your personality. Don't feel like this is set in stone either. You can absolutely change (or test) your pricing model down the road.

I will tell you what I do personally after having used both methods. There are successful designers who use both strategies so again, in the end pick what suits you and your niche.

I personally have found the most success charging by the project and then by the hour with maintenance tasks after launch. I have found the *my* customers tend to be happier this way because they know exactly what to expect and there are no surprises down the road (even if they are the ones who brought on the surprise). I have also tested out only using the per project approach except when I can tell I have a difficult customer on my hand. I can use the hourly rate as a nice way to scare them off if I really don't want to work with them or I can use it simply because I can tell the customer is going to be a lot of "work" to manage. Over the years, I just don't take on these customers anymore because it always ends up in lost money and time.

So enough about all this, what should my rate be?

Just as I would tell a web design customer, I'm going to tell you - *it depends*. But I won't leave you hanging. Let me give you some pointers.

If you follow my advice and focus on a specific niche, your rate can continually grow at a rate much faster than other designers who don't specialize. You'll be sought after by those in that industry and you'll be seen as an "expert" much faster. When focusing on a specific niche, I also hope you will focus (at least initially) on a specific (local) geographic area. This will really help you target customers and get projects faster. At the same time it can better help you determine your rate.

Here are a few ideas for how to determine your specific rate:

▸ Contact 3+ web designers in your local area and request a quote for a specific website you have detailed out. Study the range of prices you receive and ask questions about how they determined the cost. This will also give you a better idea of what your potential customers are seeing when they are searching for a web designer.

▸ Use one of the several calculators online that can help you determine your hourly rate (which in turn can help you price your packages). Here are a few you may want to play around with:

> http://motivapp.com/freelance-hourly-rate-calculator
>
> http://allindiewriters.com/freelance-hourly-rate-calculator/
>
> MyPrice - paid iPhone app

▸ Go to local networking meetings and speak with other web designers. Let them know you are looking for others in your area to refer Customers to when your plate gets too full. Ask about their rates to see what others in your area are charging.

To give you some specific numbers, $35/hour is on the lower end and $100/hour is on the higher end. This of course will vary depending on your location.

Understanding the Work Involved With Each Project So You Can Finish Projects Fast

Taking the time to fully understand the work involved with each project is going to make a huge difference on how quickly you finish your project, how happy your customer is and the overall quality of the end web site or product.

Not taking the time to understand what your customer is looking for is setting yourself up for failure. It will take you more time to complete a project because your customer thinks you know what they are looking for it and when you don't deliver they will continuously come back with new requests.

This is fairly easy to avoid. Of course you are going to want to sign a contract with them which we are about to get to but there are series of questions that you want to ask every customer you have to make sure you both are on the same page. So let's take a look at some of those questions.

In one form or another, I ask every single new customer to tell me about their business as if I was one of their new customers. This accomplishes two things: 1) it gives me a better understanding of their business so I can set-up their website for success and 2) it allows them an opportunity to talk about themself and their business which makes them like you more and starts them on the road to being one of my very happy customers.

I have pulled together a document of the top questions I ask new customers and I have included that in the appendix of this book. I don't necessarily ask every single customer every single question, but this gives me something to work off of. I have this printed off and I keep this pinned next to my phone so I don't miss anything.

Let's look at a few of the top questions:

1. Tell me more about your business (it's a good idea to ask at least a few follow-up questions as well).

2. When visitors arrive on your website, what are the top two (or three) things you would like them to do?

3. What do you hope to achieve with your new website?

4. When would you like to launch your new website?

5. Can you show me 2-3 websites related to your work or not and what you like about each one (color scheme, navigation, layout, a particular feature, etc.)? *Note: I typically ask Customers to email me this list so they have time to think about it. This question is huge and I ask EVERY SINGLE Customer this question. It gives me a better idea of what they're looking for so I can design the website for their taste and not my own.*

Once you have a better understanding of what's involved you will be able to put together a proposal for the Customer.

Creating a Web Design Proposal the Customer Can't Resist

It's very exciting to get a new project and even more exciting when the customer is excited and wants you to get started NOW! But...don't let your emotions get the best of you. I guarantee you'll be sorry at some point. Even in the off chance this project goes smoothly, that customer will refer someone who will expect the <u>same</u> treatment and then things get a little messed up.

Have a process and stick to it. Period. You'll thank me (and yourself) later.

A proposal is a quick outline of the project with three main parts:

1. A detailed description of the work to be done
2. A timeline for project completion
3. A project quote

Now these three points are fairly straightforward. These are the three things every customer will want to know. I have included an example project proposal in the appendix. *Side note: always have your own attorney look at any contracts you hand out to customers before using them.*

From experience, I highly recommend you also include a note about how long you will honor the proposal. You don't have to make a big deal about this but including in the proposal will do a couple of things for you. First, it will light a little fire under your customer because they will realize the price could change and they should act now. Secondly, (and yes, although this is not the norm I've had this happen on a couple of occassions) you can easily change your price (or service) down the road if the customer takes the proposal, disappears off the face of the earth and then returns a year later saying they're ready to get started. At that point they will likely be expecting a price increase and you won't have to think about whether increasing the price will lose you the job.

You shouldn't be spending much time writing a proposal because each one should be relatively the same. With a niche selected you've been able to easily identify which features almost every site you offer will have. They may look different but the backend work will be mostly the same. Just tweak the customer name, a feature or two, the price and deadline and boom, you're done.

Takes 5 minutes.

Now back to completing your other projects, finding new ones and providing great customer service.

Creating a Final Contract for Hassle Free Projects = More Money

After the new customer is happy with the proposal, you'll want to send them a final contract - which I like to call a final agreement. It just sounds a little nicer and less intimidating although it definitely includes all the important pieces. It's like calling a "budget" a "spending plan." Spending plan sounds more fun and is definitely less intimidating. Same thing here. Definitely not something you have to do. It's just my personal preference that I wanted to share with you.

The final agreement (or contract) includes all the same parts as your proposal plus a few additional important points.

1. Needed materials

2. Payment terms

3. Fees & additional services

4. And a handful of other (important) sections with some legal jargon

I'm sure you wondering why I don't choose to include this in the initial proposal. Well, here's why. I want the customer to make the decision to go with me as quickly as possible. After they've already made the decision in their mind, then we can discuss the last few details to get started. This part tends to go very quickly and easily. I also don't want to overwhelm a new customer immediately which can send them running in the other direction.

Let's break down some of these sections a bit.

The needed materials section includes a list of everything the customer must provide you with in order for you to start the project. It is imperative to your success that you get these materials BEFORE you start the project. If you don't I guarantee your project will get dragged out and the customer will have more time to ask you for changes and updates. Save yourself the headache and get everything upfront.

In the payment terms section a deposit of some sort should be requested. Serious buyers / customers expect this as you are providing a professional service. I always request a deposit (in my case it's 25% but you can do more or less) before getting started. I have found this always separates the non-serious buyers from the serious buyers.

Those who are willing to put their money where their mouth is are WAY more likely to 1) get you the needed materials quickly, 2) provide feedback on your work quickly, 3) ask for less new requests and 4) pay the remaining amount on time.

If you don't believe me, try not requesting a deposit for awhile and you'll see how much longer you spend on projects and how much more of a headache the customers you work with are.

Just as with the proposal you'll want to include a deadline for how long you will honor the quote.

The fees and additional services section can be short and sweet but it's very important. Here is where you will inform customers that you will not be doing free work if they want to change the scope of the project after you get started. To be honest, you'll probably slip in a few minor free changes along the way but it keeps the customer happy and gives you an opportunity to remind them of what they'll be charged if they request additional changes.

You'll find a sample final agreement in the appendix to help get you started. You'll also find a separate document with the same agreement that provides explanations of each section. Look that over carefully and if you plan to use those documents, make sure to consult your attorney.

The Secrets to Easy Customer Communication

Establishing a Process that Will Help You Finish Projects Quickly = More Money

As I've already briefly mentioned, you'll want to establish a process for how you do your work. It will keep you (and your team - if you have one) more organized, allowing you to complete projects faster and ultimately make more money.

I have a general process that walks customers through the "stages" of my service so they know what to expect. This helps educate them on how I work and it also helps me look more professional.

See the appendix for a copy of a general web design process you can use for customers. Feel free to use this and tweak it for your needs.

I also have an internal process for myself (and my team) to help us know where we are with each project and to help us complete each project quickly and accurately. An internal process for me comes in the form of a checklist (but you can set-up whatever format works best for your working style) and includes these parts:

1. List of tasks (install WordPress, install standard plugins, create new pages, send demo to customer, etc.)

2. A list of the plugins used for all customers (feature niche-specific plugins, SEO plugins, contact form plugin, etc.)

As you start to grow you will be thankful if you already have a process in place to help keep you organized so you can shift between projects easily without losing time trying to figure out where you left off. It also helps provide customer updates quickly and gives the customer the impression they are always on the top of your list and you are on top of your game.

You'll find an example checklist in the appendix which will give you a general idea of what your internal process can look like. Tweak it for your specific niche and you've got your process in place! It is created in excel so you can create a new tab for each customer / project you have and can easily switch between projects as you speak with customers and complete your work.

Establishing Expectations for Both Parties & Staying in Control of the Process

Following a process (or not following a process) will make or break your long-term success. Sure, you'll find work but we want to make things as easy as possible for ourselves. Staying in control of each project will not only make you look more professional (and like you know what you are doing) but you'll also notice your projects will go much, much smoother.

I cannot emphasize this enough. The last thing you want is for your customer to take control. Now don't get me wrong. I don't mean for you to come off like you are the end-all-be-all. Simply keeping professional control will keep both you and the customer happier.

Ok, sounds good, but how do I do this? There are a handful of tactics that will make the customer defer to you instead of being more demanding and trying to fight you for control of the project:

1. Start with your initial conversation. Share you expertise, share your process and always ask the questions we talked about earlier.

2. Use a proposal and agreement (contract) that tells the customer what to expect and show them this is a two way street. You, as the web designer, will have expectations of them as the customer and they, as the customer, will have expectations of you as the web designer.

3. Have a process (as we talked about in the last section) and stick to it.

4. Update the customer on your progress with their website before they are expecting it and before they ask. Once I have part of a website set-up, I always send customers a demo URL where they can see their website being built. This makes them feel more comfortable because they don't have to take your word on what's been done. I do ask them to not provide feedback initially because it's still a work in progress and I inform them I will request feedback at certain points once some features have been completed. This keeps them happy while at the same time, it keeps them from freaking out because things appear a bit out of whack initially.

5. Stay on top of your communication with each customer. Not getting back to them in a timely manner seems to give them the idea they can expect more.

Staying in control and establishing expectations for your customer (and yourself - don't make this all about them. Show them what you'll bring to the table too) is all about communication.

How to Be Successful Long-Term: Completing the Project & Cashing In

Handling New Customer Requests Without Losing Your Mind

As I said in the very beginning of this book, I didn't write this book to tell you what you *want* to hear, I wrote this book to tell you what you need to know. And you need to know that you will likely never work on a project with a customer who doesn't even request one change / update to what you've done.

So go into every project expecting it.

That doesn't mean you have to just do everything a customer requests of you but rather you should be prepared to handle it. With every project you complete, you'll gain more experience in helping the customer in the initial stage identify exactly what it is that they want you to do and how to best handle new requests that are not mentioned in your final contract. But since you're not there quite yet, I want to start you off with a few tips so you don't have to learn the hard way.

1. We already covered detailing exactly what you will be doing in the proposal and final contract. If you only walk away with one tip, use this one.

2. As we'll discuss more in a few moments, go ahead and complete 1-2-3 small, non-time consuming changes the customer requests. Use that as an opportunity to remind the customer the changes are outside the initial scope of work and you will have to bill for new changes. This is very effective. They feel like you are being reasonable for throwing in a few changes and they won't expect more.

3. If larger changes or additions are requested, inform the customer that it is outside the initial scope of work and suggest you look into it once the original work has been completed. Once you've completed the initial work you can see if the customer is even still interested in the work to be completed and if they are you can provide them with a separate quote for that work.

If you handle new customer requests like a pro, you'll always finish projects much, much faster and your revenue will reflect that.

Save Yourself Time: Customer Testing, Final Feedback & Approval

Once a project is completed it's time to have the customer test the website, provide their final feedback and approve the work you have done. As I am nearing completion, I like to shoot the customer a quick email to let them know I am close to completing everything and inform them I will be asking them to test the website and provide some final feedback. If you can provide the customer the date you will be requesting their feedback, they will expect it and will be hopefully be setting aside some time to take a look at your work.

When requesting the final feedback from the customer there are a few things to ask them to do. First, ask them to complete all the forms on the website (contact form, newsletter sign-up form, quote form, etc.). They should make sure they work correctly and check to make sure they receive a notice in their inbox that the form(s) has been filled out. Customers should also be asked to go through the website (and each page) as a website visitor would and provide any last/final feedback for changes they would like to see.

Side note: if a customer asks for text/content changes, I use this as an opportunity to show them how to do it themselves since it is the customer's responsibility to provide the site's content and I always walk through how to manage the website anyways.

For websites that include an online store, appointment scheduling feature or other larger / non-standard feature, the customer should be asked to walk through the entire process just as a potential website visitor would so they can see how it works.

Provide a specific date and time for the customer to return their final feedback to you. Twenty-four to forty-eight hours is a good general timeframe for this. You should try and not spend more than 24-48 hours yourself implementing the final feedback (as long as it's reasonable of course) before informing the customer the final changes have been completed and a launch date can be scheduled.

Once the project has been approved by your customer, I recommend launching as quickly as possible to minimize the chance of the customer requesting any new changes since they've had even longer to look at the website and it hasn't yet gone live. At the same time I would recommend scheduling the launch date for earlier in the week if possible. Launching late Thursday or on Friday can cause frantic weekend emails and phone calls when a bug is discovered on the site and you're at home relaxing with your family. Avoid the end of the week if possible.

Some customers may request a specific launch date and if they request a Friday or even a weekend launch, don't be afraid to let them know when you can be available (if at all) and even possibly charge for some higher-rate weekend work to make sure you're available.

Training Customers on Their Website So You Can Concentrate On Making More Money

After launching a website, schedule a time within the next 2-3 days max to train the customer how to manage the website. This training can be conducted via phone or skype. At this time I walk customers step-by-step through how to edit text, upload images, change a sidebar item, etc. I also choose to provide them with written step-by-step instructions on how to complete these changes (see the appendix for an example guide you can tweak and provide each customer). Often times customers still request I do the updates anyway and other times it saves me from stopping work on a profitable project to do a 15-minute maintenance text update on another site. Simply not worth the time.

Anything you can do to eliminate customers asking for text and image updates will ultimately earn you more money. If it takes you 5-minutes to change the text it's not a big deal but you've taken your focus off other big projects and marketing which lead to more money. You may even consider creating quick how-to videos you can simply point customers to.

Remember, when it comes to really minor website maintenance tasks...let's chase dollars not pennies!

The Secret to Keeping You and Your Customers Happy

The Ticket to Keeping Customers Happy (While Still Keeping Yourself Happy)

If you want to survive long term in this field, there is nothing I can recommend more than finding a balance between keeping both your customers and yourself happy. This isn't always an easy task but by following what I've outlined in this book, you'll be well on your way to making this a reality.

Here are some simple things you can do to make your customers happy while keeping yourself happy and making your life easier at the same time:

▸ For every project, plan on adding some "freebies" to the website that were not discussed or quoted for. This could be something as simple as installing an extra SEO plugin or statistics dashboard plugin that will make the customer feel like they got something extra but in reality it only took you 5 minutes to do. This often spurs future work and referrals to new customers. That will always make your life easier!

▸ If a customer requests updates to their website before launch that were not agreed upon, take 1, 2 or even 3 that will only take you a matter of minutes to do. Let the customer know you've done them at "no additional charge," followed by a reminder that future non-agreed upon changes will be billed at the standard rate. The customer is happy they got something for free and you've established a boundary you likely won't have to deal with again.

▸ Say no...it's okay to do it nicely. Customers will try anything they can to get you to work for them for as long as possible at no additional expense to them. If they ask for something outrageous, it's okay to simply say no. Letting a customer know you would be more than happy to complete the work and would be happy to provide them with a separate quote is fine. If you reviewed the final contract with them, there should be no surprise. Don't be afraid of this. After all if you went to buy a new car and as you were about to walk off the lot said, "hey, could you just add a sun roof real quick?" You'd better bet they'll do it...but you'll be paying for it.

Doing something you may not normally otherwise for a favorite customer or someone who has been nice to work with may not seem like a big deal but I'd still advise against it. Once you do it, the customer then expects it moving forward. It makes them happy so they refer their friends to you but then they tell them what you did for free and now that person expects it. It can get out of control quickly. Stick with these tips and what you've learned thus far. I promise you, you'll be happy you did.

11 Ways to Get Repeat Work & Referrals Without Asking

The easiest and fastest way for getting repeat customers, getting referrals and increasing your revenue without any extra effort on your part, no doubt starts with your great customer service. I know, there I go bringing that up good ol' customer customer again...but it's seriously that important to your success.

Since these tips have been sprinkled throughout this book (although I've added some new ones below), I'll quickly recap:

1. Use the tactics mentioned in the previous section - keeping customers happy

2. Do a little something extra on every project the customer isn't expecting (you'd be surprised at how excited a customer can be about something extra they got for free that only took you 5 minutes to do - although they don't have to know that part!)

3. Have a referral program and include it in your email signature, homepage or sidebar of your website or even a newsletter you send out, with an incentive for referring others.

4. At a minimum, complete each project on time if not ahead of schedule.

5. Respond to customers as quickly as possible. Same day is best (although not always possible).

6. Do what you can to support your customer's business. Attend an event they have, refer a friend to them or purchase an inexpensive product from them.

7. Be personable. It only takes a few extra minutes to ask someone about their weekend, their family or just how they're doing. Do your best to make the conversation about the customer if you can since people love talking about themselves and they end up liking you more in the end for listening to them.

8. Don't sugar coat anything. Be very straightforward in your communication with customers. They'll know exactly what to expect, the process will go smoothly and everyone involved will end up happy.

9. Update each customer on the progress of their website before they are expecting it and before they ask. This shows you are on the ball and are a professional who knows what they're doing.

10. Offer free information by posting new articles on your website or sending out a general newsletter. It establishes you as more of an expert and you'll remind them of (probably unrelated) work they needed done.

11. Follow-up. After a new website has launched, follow-up with the customer after a week to see how things are going. It'll be a nice unexpected surprise and only add to their satisfaction with you and your service.

Following what I've outlined for you in this book will get you repeat work and referrals. I guarantee it.

11 Upsells for Every Web Design Customer

The best way to increase your income month after month is to upsell your current customers. Whatever you can do to *save* time finding new customers is going to increase your revenue and that's what we're after here. We've already talked about how to get repeat work and referrals. Let's shift our focus here and look at what else you can sell to your customer (upsells). Some of these upsells can be agreed upon at the same time you sign-up a customer for your web design service while others may be sold after their website is complete. Let's take a look at what you can offer:

1. Website maintenance packages
    For customers who want you to manage their site you can offer them a discounted hourly rate if they pay you upfront for a specific number of hours per month. The more hours they purchase, the lower the rate. To keep things simple, let's say your hourly rate is $50 / hour. If they pay you on the 1st of every month for 5 hours of website maintenance you may drop your rate to $45 or $43 per hour. If they purchase 10 hours it will drop even lower. Then they can send you updates throughout the month and you'll take care of it.

2. Hosting packages
    Many web designers offer web hosting services as a way to generate some additional monthly revenue. It's a great idea and there are two ways this can be done. Option 1: Many hosting companies sell a reseller package which allows you to appear as if you own your own hosting company as well and sell space on their services. You pay a monthly fee to *rent* the space and you can charge customers whatever monthly fee you'd like. Option 2: you can refer customers to a hosting company as an affiliate and earn money for the referral.

    With option 1, if your customer's website goes down (and at some point it will) because servers need maintenance, they crash, etc. - you'd better bet they're going to call you. And they won't keep in mind what day of the week it is or what time it is. If you go with option 2, once you've made the referral, you're done.

3. Logo design
    This is pretty straightforward. If a customer comes to you with a very outdated logo or a brand new business, it's time to sell them a new logo!

4. Print design
    Many business owners need business cards at least, if not additional marketing materials such as postcards, brochures, etc. Offer to design their marketing materials for them.

5. Search engine optimization
    Everybody wants to be number one on Google and have visitors flooding their website. Two suggestions: first, if you know about this (or take the time to learn), this is a great monthly recurring income stream. Second, if you don't know SEO (or don't want to learn about it), consider partnering with someone who does this service and work out a referral fee for every customer you send their way. *Just make sure they don't offer web design services too or you may lose out down the road!*

6. Email marketing services
    Just as you may send out an e-newsletter, your customers may want to do so as well. Although this is a very good marketing technique, a lot of people don't have or make the time to do it. Offer to put together their newsletter for them and send it out so they don't have to worry about it.

7. In-person trainings (one-on-one or group) for content management systems (WordPress, Joomla, etc.)
    You may have equipped your customer with some basic written instructions for updating their website and even walked them through how to make some changes over the phone. If a customer would like some additional personalized training or if a group of people will all be updating the website, offer individual or group in-person trainings.

8. Regular website backups
    Every website should be backed up on a regular basis. The actually frequency depends on how often they update their website and how much content they are okay with losing should their files ever be lost due to hacking or another cause. Both files and databases need to be backed-up to fully restore a website.

9. Website add-ons (new features)
   Especially if you're focusing on a particular niche, if you find a new feature for one customer, you likely can use it for all your other customers. Send a notice to everyone letting them know how this new website feature will benefit their business and their bottom line and see how many customers you can get to say *"yes, please!"*

10. Content writing
    I require customers provide their own website content but sometimes a customer would like additional content added to their website about a variety of topics. If your customer does not have any website content or would like new content, offer to write it for them.

11. Photography
    You may be wondering why I'm including this here. The truth is, images can truly make or break a site. I can't tell you how many times I've designed a great looking site, only to have a customer replace it will some blurry, pixelated images down the road, making the website look awful in my opinion. Many customers don't have good pictures of their storefront, products, etc. This is where you can step in!

12. Promote affiliate products
    Ok, so this is an extra one since it's not really an upsell. Writing about (or talking about) affiliate products where you earn a commission if the customer ends up buying the product. Again, this will be easier if you can focus on products that pertain to a particular niche. Add affiliate products to a resource page on your website, within articles on your website or even in your e-newsletter.

I'm sure for at least one or two of these points you're thinking - *but I don't know how to do 'x.'* You don't have to offer all of these upsells to every customer and you also don't have to do all of these yourself. Focus on what you do best and outsource the rest (you can always expand your services as you grow. Don't feel like you have to incorporate everything right now).

Finding Customers to Get Your Business Off the Ground

13 Free Ways to Find New Website Design Customers & More Work

With everything you've learned, it won't mean a thing unless you are able to find customers to get you started. Here are some places you can look for customers:

1. Use online marketplaces such as Elance.com or Odesk.com.

2. Respond to ads for work on Craigslist.com.

3. Optimize your website for search engines. It shouldn't be too hard to rank if you are serving a particular niche in a specific geographic area.

4. If you focus on hair salons in Austin, Texas for example, visit the salons and speak to the manager. If they say no, ask them if they know of anyone who may be able to use your service.

5. Post videos on YouTube to increase traffic and leads to your website.

6. Tell everyone you know about your new service and use any connections you can find.

7. Add yourself to local business directories to help be found online.

8. Join local networking events in the industry you will be serving.

9. Set-up a profile on LinkedIn and start connecting with others immediately.

10. Use SearchTempest to find job postings in your local area that meet your skill set.

11. Set-up a referral program with incentives and promote it.

12. Create a freebie and give it away online and in-person. This could be a free guide or eBook you've created that teaches people how to make more sales with their website and of course this should point them to contacting you.

13. The number one way to get more work faster is by looking to your current customers and getting referrals. Nothing is better. Period.

Examples of How to Achieve $1,000+ Per Month With Your Services

If your goal is to make $1,000 a month this can easily be accomplished even if you're only doing this part time. Use the scenarios below to think about how you would like to achieve the $1,000 per month mark and how you can scale it if your goal is $1,500, $2,000, $2,500, etc. per month. This will help you focus your marketing efforts to achieve your financial goals.

Here are some possible scenarios depending on the rates you charge that could easily get you to $1,000 per month:

Scenario 1: sell one website per month at $1,000

Scenario 2: sell two websites per month at $500 each

Scenario 3: sell only 1 small website for $500 and sign-up two website maintenance customers at 5 hours per month

Scenario 4: sell 1 website per month at $500 - $700 and sell various upsells or website maintenance to equal the remaining amount.

Sample Web Design Business Documents For You to Use In Your Business

Below you'll find at list of all of the documents that were mentioned in the book.

*** A note about using the sample documents in this book:*

All of the documents provided in this book are free for you to tweak and use in your own business. You should not use these exactly as is but rather use them as a guide. Tweak them so they resemble your own business.

None of these documents should be considered legal documents and whenever you present documents to customers to be signed, you should first have them looked at by your own attorney. I presented these as a guide for you to use based on what I have used but I cannot take responsibility for your use of them especially as you tweak them and send them to clients in different locations.

I do hope they help you and give you a good place to start. As always, if you have any questions please do not hesitate to ask!

**Web Site Design and Development Proposal
for *Client's Business Name***

My goal is to ensure you, the Client, is delighted with my service. One way I accomplish this is by making sure both parties have a clear understanding of what is to be expected. This proposal outlines the work to be done, the timeline for completing the project and the project quote.

Description of Work

The purpose of this project is to create a professional, modern and user-friendly website for Client Business Name. This will be achieved with the work as outlined below:

Web Design & Development

The new Client Business Name website design and development package will include the following:

▸ A design template that reflects the work of Client Business Name.

▸ A Content Management System (WordPress) to update content without   knowledge of web coding. The Content Management System will allow you to:

- Add/Delete/Edit text and images within the content pages (and blog posts)

- Add/Delete/Edit menus and submenus

- Add/Delete/Edit content pages

- Update the items on your sidebar

▸ Photo Gallery for displaying images of events, etc. The photo gallery will allow you to:

- Add/Delete/Edit images

- Create and display new galleries

- Set-up of up to 10 pages of content
- A contact form
- A newsletter sign-up box to collect customer email addresses (using 'Aweber/MailChimp/Other service)
- Social media sharing icons displayed on pages and posts (if desired)
- Search Engine Optimization (SEO) friendly pages
- Google Analytics Integration (free website statistics)
- Phone training to learn how to use the Content Management System to make changes to the site
- Written instructions for using the Content Management System

Needed Materials

The following is a list of materials needed in order to start the project:

- List of 3 or more sample websites with what you like and dislike about the site (navigation, layout, color scheme, etc.)
- High resolution log
- All content to be included on site pages (including blog posts)
- Menu items (home, about us, services, programs, contact us, etc.) and submenu items
- Any images to be used in the design of the website, if any
- All images for the photo gallery and list of categories for photo gallery
- Newsletter information
- Google Analytics account information (if currently in use)
- FTP & hosting account information

Timeline for Project Completion

The project as described above in the description of work will be completed within 7 to 10 days assuming the Client is available to provide feedback to the Service Company on a daily basis.

Your Business Name will provide support for fixing website bugs (not caused by the client) and answering questions related to how to use the new website for 30 days after website launch at no additional charge.

Project Quote

Web Design and Development (as outlined above) .... $X,XXX

This quote is guaranteed until MM/DD/YY.

Sample Web Design Contract

Web Site Design and Development Agreement

My goal is to ensure you, the Client, is delighted with my service. One way I accomplish this is by making sure both parties have a clear understanding of what is to be expected. This agreement outlines both what you as the Client can expect from me and what I as the Service Company can expect from you.

Description of Work

The purpose of this project is to create a professional, modern and user-friendly website for Client Business Name. This will be achieved with the work as outlined below:

Web Design & Development

The new Client Business Name website design and development package will include the following:

▸ A design template that reflects the work of Client Business Name.

▸ Content Management System (WordPress) to update content without knowledge of web coding. The Content Management System will allow you to:

- Add/Delete/Edit text and images within the content pages (and blog posts)

- Add/Delete/Edit menus and submenus

- Add/Delete/Edit content pages

- Update the items on your sidebar

▸ Photo Gallery for displaying images of events, etc. The photo gallery will allow you to:

- Add/Delete/Edit images

- Create and display new galleries

- Set-up of up to 10 pages of content

- A contact form

- A newsletter sign-up box to collect customer email addresses (using 'Aweber MailChimp/Other service)

- Social media sharing icons displayed on pages and posts (if desired)

- Search Engine Optimization (SEO) friendly pages

- Google Analytics Integration (free website statistics)

- Phone training to learn how to use the Content Management System to make changes to the site

- Written instructions for using the Content Management System

Any work not described above will be quoted separately.

Timeline

The project as described above in the description of work will be completed within 7 to 10 days assuming the Client is available to provide feedback to the Service Company on a daily basis. Each day the Client is unavailable to provide feedback may push the project completion date back by one day. Failure to submit required information or materials as outlined below may cause delays in the production. Please provide additional time for client feedback.

Your Business Name will provide support for fixing website bugs (not caused by the client) and answering questions related to how to use the new website for 30 days after website launch at no additional cost.

Needed Materials

The following is a list of needed materials in order to start the project:

- List of 3 or more sample websites with what you like and dislike about the site (navigation, layout, color scheme, etc.)

- High resolution logo

- All content to be included on site pages (including blog posts)
- Menu items (home, about us, services, programs, contact us, etc.) and submenu items
- Any images to be used in the design of the website, if any
- All images for the photo gallery and list of categories for photo gallery
- Newsletter information
- Google Analytics account information (if currently in use)
- FTP & hosting account information

Payment Terms

Web Design and Development as described above.................................... $ X,XXX

A 25% deposit for the web design and development work of $XXX is due at the start of the project. The remaining balance of $XXX is due immediately upon website completion and upload to the Client's server.

This quote is guaranteed until MM/DD/YY.

Fees & Additional Services

Any work which is not specified in the description of work above will be considered an additional service and will require a separate agreement and payment from what is included in this agreement. Excessive change requests will be charged separately at the hourly rate of $XX.

Authorization

The Client, Client Business Name, is engaging Your Business Name as the Service Company to develop a website that is to be installed on the Client's server upon completion. The Client hereby authorizes the Service Company to access this account for the purposes of developing and maintaining the website to be created.

Confidentiality

The Client and Service Company may disclose confidential information one to the other to facilitate work under this Agreement. Such information shall be so identified in writing at the time of its transmittal, and shall be safeguarded and not disclosed to third parties by the receiving party.

Permissions and Releases

The Client agrees to indemnify and hold harmless the Service Company against any and all claims, costs, and expenses, including attorney's fees, due to materials included in the Work at the request of the Client for which no copyright permission or previous release was requested or uses which exceed the uses allowed pursuant to a permission or release.

Termination

Either party may terminate this Agreement by giving 30 days written notice to the other of such termination. In the event that Work is postponed or terminated at the request of the Client, the Service Company shall have the right to bill pro rata for work completed through the date of that request, while reserving all rights under this Agreement. If additional payment is due, this shall be payable within thirty days of the Client's written notification to stop work. In the event of termination, the Service Company shall own all rights to the Work. The Client shall assume responsibility for all collection of legal fees necessitated by default in payment.

The undersigned agrees to the terms of this agreement on behalf of his or her organization or business.

On behalf of the Client:
(Signature & Print Name)
Date:

Your Business Name:
(Signature & Print Name)
Date:

Sample Web Design Contract (With Detailed Explanations on Each Section)

Web Site Design and Development Agreement

This document includes explanations in red to better explain the pieces of this agreement. This agreement can be modified to meet your needs but gives you a good idea of what should be included.

My goal is to ensure you, the Client, is delighted with my service. One way I accomplish this is by making sure both parties have a clear understanding of what is to be expected. This agreement outlines both what you as the Client can expect from me and what I as the Service Company can expect from you.

This helps client's take some ownership in the process and demonstrates that you're trying to make this a partnership to deliver the work they're looking for.

Description of Work

The purpose of this project is to create a professional, modern and user-friendly website for Client Business Name. This will be achieved with the work as outlined below:

<u>Web Design & Development</u>

This is a critical section to your success. You'll want to list absolutely all tasks and features here, no matter how small. This will one, demonstrate to the client that you understand their needs and are on the same page and two, have a document to refer back to when the client says "I thought you were going to add feature x, y or z…"

The new *Client Business Name* website design and development package will include the following:

- ▸ A design template that reflects the work of Client Business Name.
- ▸ Content Management System (WordPress) to update content without knowledge of web coding. The Content Management System will allow you to:

- Add/Delete/Edit text and images within the content pages (and blog posts)
  - Add/Delete/Edit menus and submenus
  - Add/Delete/Edit content pages
  - Update the items on your sidebar
▸ Photo Gallery for displaying images of events, etc. The photo gallery will allow you to:
  - Add/Delete/Edit images
  - Create and display new galleries
▸ Set-up of up to 10 pages of content
▸ A contact form
▸ A newsletter sign-up box to collect customer email addresses (using 'Aweber/MailChimp/Other service)
▸ Social media sharing icons displayed on pages and posts (if desired)
▸ Search Engine Optimization (SEO) friendly pages
▸ Google Analytics Integration (free website statistics)
▸ Phone training to learn how to use the Content Management System to make changes to the site
▸ Written instructions for using the Content Management System

Any work not described above will be quoted separately.

The above sentence is also very important. You want to make sure they agree that they have to pay if they decide to add to the project after you've already started.

Timeline

The project as described above in the description of work will be completed within 7 to 10 days assuming the Client is available to provide feedback to the Service Company on a daily basis. Each day the Client is unavailable to provide feedback may push the project completion date back by one day. Failure to submit required information or materials as outlined below may cause delays in the production. Please provide additional time for client feedback.

Your Business Name will provide support for fixing website bugs (not caused by the client) asnd answering questions related to how to use the new website for 30 days after website launch at no additional cost.

The timeline section is important for four reasons:

1) You identify how long it will take you to complete the project

2) You let the client know they must make themselves available during the project for questions and feedback or the completion date will be delayed

3) You have the opportunity to overdeliver by telling the client you will complete the website in 'X' number of days / weeks and quietly aim for a sooner date so they will be thrilled when you deliver early. This helps with repeat work down the road and referrals to colleagues.

4) Clients occassionally mess up their websites some how or they find things wrong (that were not their fault). If you don't have the last paragraph in your contract, it can make it hard to decide when to charge and when not to charge when they come back to you. Personally, I prefer a client to begin testing their site immediately as bugs can happen anytime. If a client comes back to me after 3 months with a bug, they are already expecting to pay for me to fix it. Without this line, I've had clients want it done for free.

Needed Materials

Perhaps the biggest thing you can do to ensure you finish your project on time, get paid on time, and eliminates the likelihood of clients requesting new features and changes due to the project taking longer than expected.

The following is a list of needed materials in order to start the project:

- List of 3 or more sample websites with what you like and dislike about the site (navigation, layout, color scheme, etc.)
- High resolution logo
- All content to be included on site pages (including blog posts)
- Menu items (home, about us, services, programs, contact us, etc.) and submenu items
- Any images to be used in the design of the website, if any
- All images for the photo gallery and list of categories for photo gallery
- Newsletter information

- ‣ Google Analytics account information (if currently in use)
- ‣ FTP & hosting account information *(if the client does have a hosting account, offer to set it up for them and use an affiliate account to generate additional revenue)*

Payment Terms

Web Design and Development as described above.. $ X,XXX

A 25% deposit for the web design and development work of $XXX is due at the start of the project. The remaining balance of $XXX is due immediately upon website completion and upload to the Client's server.

Charging an upfront deposit (even a small one) is a good idea for several reasons:

It separates the serious clients from not serious ones
It helps make sure you'll get the remaining payment at the end of the project
It helps get the client more serious about and more involved in the process

This quote is guaranteed until MM/DD/YY.

Adding a small note about how long you'll honor the quote is a good idea for two reasons:

1. *It creates urgency*
2. *It will help you increase the price when a client returns a year later and tells you they are ready to begin the project. This has happened to me a few times where clients have returned a year later to my surprise telling me they are ready to begin. By that time I have changed my pricing and had to decide whether to raise the price and potentially lose the work or work at a lower price than what I want to.*

Fees & Additional Services

Any work which is not specified in the description of work above will be considered an additional service and will require a separate agreement and payment from what is included in this agreement. Excessive change requests will be charged separately at the hourly rate of $XX.

This is written losely allowing you to permit some small changes while reminding the client that additional changes will be billed for. Almost all clients will ask for some small changes and I always plan to complete a couple for them to keep them happy while letting them know I have to bill for additional features / tasks. 99% of the time they are more than happy with that arrangement.

Authorization

The Client, *Client Business Name*, is engaging *Your Business Name* as the Service Company to develop a website that is to be installed on the Client's server upon completion. The Client hereby authorizes the Service Company to access this account for the purposes of developing and maintaining the website to be created.

Confidentiality

The Client and Service Company may disclose confidential information one to the other to facilitate work under this Agreement. Such information shall be so identified in writing at the time of its transmittal, and shall be safeguarded and not disclosed to third parties by the receiving party.

Permissions and Releases

The Client agrees to indemnify and hold harmless the Service Company against any and all claims, costs, and expenses, including attorney's fees, due to materials included in the Work at the request of the Client for which no copyright permission or previous release was requested or uses which exceed the uses allowed pursuant to a permission or release.

The above three sections protect you from any issues that can arise through no fault of your own. Especially when clients request you use certain images, you want to make sure they own the images. This paragraph will protect you if they do provide you with images they don't have the rights to.

Termination

Either party may terminate this Agreement by giving 30 days written notice to the other of such termination. In the event that Work is postponed or terminated at the request of the Client, the Service Company shall have the right to bill pro rata for work completed through the date of that request, while reserving all rights under this Agreement. If additional payment is due, this shall be payable within thirty days of the Client's written notification to stop work. In the event of termination, the Service Company shall own all rights to the Work. The Client shall assume responsibility for all collection of legal fees necessitated by default in payment.

In all my years of doing things as I've presented in these documents and on this site, I've never had a client terminate a contract. The only times this has ever happened is when a contract was not in place and I did not stay on top of the client like I advise here. In the event a termination happens, this is important to ensure you still receive payment.

The undersigned agrees to the terms of this agreement on behalf of his or her organization or business.

On behalf of the Client:
(Signature & Print Name)
Date:

Your Business Name:
(Signature & Print Name)
Date:

After the client signs the agreement and sends it back to you, make sure to sign it and give them a copy for their records to refer back to. You never want to have a disagreement and them not have the contract available to them.

Website Planning Guide /
Client Questionnaire

Creating a new website or redesigning your current one can be an overwhelming task. We're here to help simplify the process. It is important to spend time before creating your website to think about what you would like to achieve with your new site. Let's get started!

Tell me about your business.

If you have a current website, start with the following questions.

Let's Talk About Your Current Site (if you have one, otherwise skip this section)

List the top three things you do not like about your current site:

1.
2.
3.

What features would you like to keep (if any)?

Do you have website statistics for your current site? Do you have a copy for your records?

Do you have a current logo you would like to use?

Let's Talk About Your Competition

Do you know who your competitors are?

What makes your products / services unique? How do you stand out from the crowd?

Let's Talk About Your New Site

What do you hope to accomplish with your new website?

Who is your target audience? Describe them as much as possible.

When a visitor arrives at your site, what would you like them to do?

Is there any new content that will need to be written for the website? Who will be responsible for that?

List three websites you like (related to your work or not) and what you like about each one (color scheme, navigation, layout, etc.). This will help us get a better idea of your taste.

Website #1:
Likes:

Website #2:
Likes:

Website #3:
Likes:

Let's Talk About Your Online Store *(for e-commerce websites only)*

How many products do you plan to sell at first?

How many products do you plan to sell in the future?

How will you handle shipping?

What payment gateway will you be using (PayPal, etc.)?

Timeframe & Budget

When would you like to launch your new website?

What is your budget for building a website?

Congratulations! You've Successfully Planned Your New Website!

Project Task List (Example Checklist With Process)

Task	Deadline	Responsible Party	Notes	Completed
Project Start				
Collect deposit				
Collect needed materials				
Set-up hosting account (affiliate?)				
Set-up demo URL				
Website Creation Process				
Install WordPress *(or other CMS)*				
Install plugins from list				
Install any extra plugins from agreement				
Set-up pages				
Set-up contact page				
Install and tweak template				
Feedback & Final Testing				
Request initial client feedback				
Final testing (test all forms, features, links, etc.)				
Request final client feedback				
Complete final feedback changes				
Wrapping It Up				
Send final payment notice				
Collect payment				
Transfer website to client's hosting				

5 Step Web Design & Development Process

Step 1: Knowledge

During the knowledge step the customer and designer discuss the mission of the business and what the company hopes to achieve with a new website.

Step 2: Layout & Design

Once the designer has a better understanding of the business, the design work begins. Based on information provided, the web designer will create a design and send it to you for review. The design is worked on until you are 100% satisfied and love the way it looks!

Step 3: Implementation

Now that we have a final design we can begin building the actual website. The implementation step consists of creating the content management system, any additional features and integrating the final design. This step is where the website comes to life and you can start using all the features.

Step 4: Feedback

Now that the website is ready we want to hear your final feedback. If there is anything that needs tweaking we will make changes before the site goes live.

Step 5: Launch & Training

The new site is ready to be shown to the world! In the launch and training step, the website is made live for customers to see. Training is available to learn how to use the new content management system so you can make changes to the website content without knowledge of web coding.

Launching Your Web Design Business Today: Your Next Steps - Start Earning Money!

Where to Download Web Design Business Documents & Special Bonuses

Due to the popularity and success of this book, the material has been turned into an online video course for easier learning. As part of the course you can also download editable versions of the business documents found within this book for you to tweak and use in your own business.

With this course you receive:

- ▸ Lifetime access to all course material
- ▸ Downloadable business documents
- ▸ Access to the instructor to ask questions and get feedback
- ▸ New material not found within this book

As a special bonus for reading this book, you can access this course at a **90% discount** here:

https://www.udemy.com/start-a-home-web-design-business-and-make-1000-per-month/?couponCode=STARTNOW

If you're interested in learning **how to create WordPress websites without any coding,** you may also be interested in the companion video course which you can access for **91% off** just for reading this book:

https://www.udemy.com/create-wordpress-website-no-coding-required/?couponCode=WEBBIZB

Starting Your Business - Your Next Steps to a Successful Web Design Business

Congratulations on completing the book. This shows you are serious about starting your own web design business. Now that you've completed the book, the next step is simply to take action.

If you do not already have experience in web design, start by learning how to set-up websites with no coding or experience required. Then start marketing your service and you'll be well on your way to earning at least $1,000 per month.

Just do a little something every day and I promise you the results will follow!

I am available for help if you have questions or concerns as you start your new business. If you'd like this direct support, please consider joining my online course which you will find details on in the previous section. There I answer questions and provide feedback on a daily basis.

I wish you all the luck in your new business!

Start a Home SEO Business & Make Monthly Recurring Income

As a web design business owner, you'll likely be asked by customers how they can get their website ranked on the first page of Google. If you'd like to be able to provide SEO services to your customers, you may be interested in my other book: *Start a Home SEO Business & Make Monthly Recurring Income.*

http://www.amazon.com/Become-SEO-Freelancer-Generate-Recurring-ebook/dp/B00Q0PJ4RO

As a bonus, here is a free preview of the book on why SEO freelancing can be so profitable:

Becoming a SEO freelancer can be so attractive because of just how easy it is to scale. I'm picking a random number here (we'll get into pricing your service later) but let's say you charge a client $300 per month. Now this customer is going to pay you month after month to rank their website and keep it ranked so with just one customer you have a recurring monthly income of $300. But next month you find only two new customers who each agree to pay you $300 per month. You are already up to $900 a month of recurring income.

Because SEO is more of an ongoing service it is easy to create recurring income this way. It is also very easy to determine what you will need to do to achieve the income you want or need.

So let's say you want to earn $3,000 per month. You can easily determine if you have a rate of $300 per month that you will need just 10 clients.

$300 / month X 10 Clients = $3,000 / month

Of course there is always the opportunity to upsell your current clients and find new clients but even if you decide not to take on new clients or to try to upsell your current clients, you'll have a base of $3,000 per month. Nice, right?

Before continuing on, take a moment to write down how much you'd like to make per month and what your goals are with this business (a pre-determined monthly income, ongoing business growth, working less by outsourcing more, etc.). With this written down it will be easier to set things up as we move forward and it will help you strategize in future sections.

Now in another section, we'll cover some additional options for making money with SEO that you may not have thought about. You can use one or multiple methods to increase your income but that's coming up soon!

If you'd like to read more and add SEO services to your business, you can grab a copy of the book here:

http://www.amazon.com/Become-SEO-Freelancer-Generate-Recurring-ebook/dp/B00Q0PJ4RO

Thank You!

Thank you so much for taking the time to read this book. I truly hope it has given you some valuable information that you can use to set-up your own home web design business.

If you have enjoyed this book and have a few extra seconds, I would greatly appreciate it if you could leave a review so others know how helpful this book has been for you.

Leaving a review is quick and easy and you can do so here:

https://www.amazon.com/review/create-review?ie=UTF8&asin=B00Q0PJ4RO

Made in the
USA
Columbia, SC